About the author

Andrea Mills is an award-winning author of more than 50 children's books and family reference titles. Her books feature a broad range of subjects, from anatomy and animals to space and sports. This self-confessed bookworm gives regular talks at schools, book fairs, and specialist events, and enjoys the ingenious questions children ask in the Q&A sessions at the end! Andrea is a big fan of the animal kingdom and has loved writing this story about our furry friends.

About the illustrator

Julia Seal knew from the age of five what she wanted to do for a living—draw pictures! After graduating with a degree in Graphic Design and Illustration, and then working in the greeting card industry, she finally moved onto her dream job, illustrating children's books. Julia brings her expertise, charm, and passion to all the books she works on, creating wonderful characters that delight young readers.

Owl and Otter

The Big Talent Show

Written by Andrea Mills
Illustrated by Julia Seal

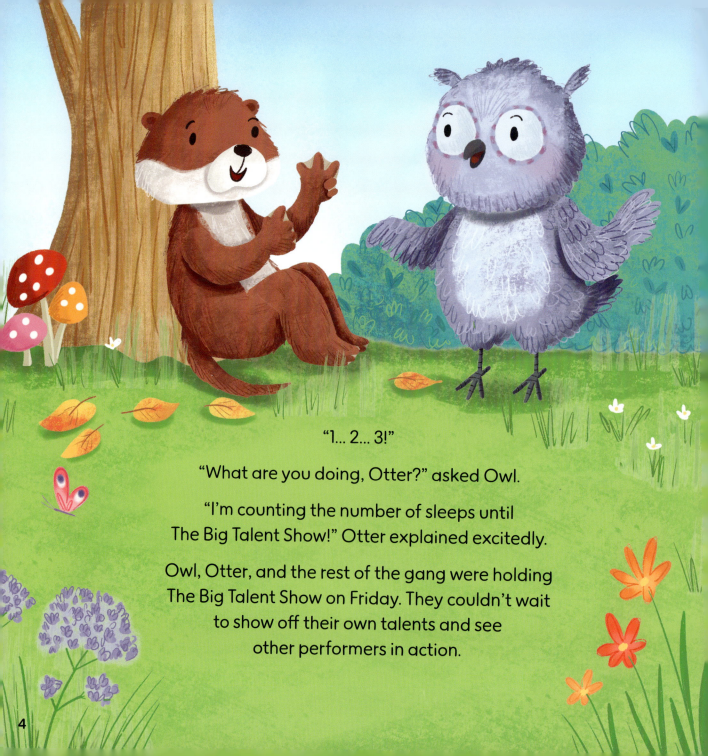

"1... 2... 3!"

"What are you doing, Otter?" asked Owl.

"I'm counting the number of sleeps until The Big Talent Show!" Otter explained excitedly.

Owl, Otter, and the rest of the gang were holding The Big Talent Show on Friday. They couldn't wait to show off their own talents and see other performers in action.

They printed 60 posters, using the savings they had left from selling cookies and lemonade at their Big Yard Sale.

The posters read:

THE BIG TALENT SHOW!

NO TALENT TOO BIG OR TOO SMALL.

EVERYONE WELCOME THIS FRIDAY.

FREE TO PERFORM. $2 TO WATCH.

Owl took charge, "Today we have to put up the posters."

Owl handed out posters to the gang. "There should be ten posters each. Can you count them to make sure?"

The group got busy counting, "1-2-3-4-5-6-7-8-9-10."

Only Woodpecker didn't have enough, "I only have nine posters, Owl. Can I have one more?"

"There's a spare one here! Nine plus one makes ten for Woodpecker." Owl gave the last poster to Woodpecker.

"Put posters up all over the neighborhood to promote the show! We want everyone to come!" explained Owl.

The friends went running and flying off. At the end of the day, everything was covered in The Big Talent Show posters.

Word soon spread about the show. By Friday, everyone was talking about it.

"No more sleeps until The Big Talent Show! It's today!" squealed Otter.

The gang set up the stage, with banners and balloons hanging from the trees. Fireflies were already showing off their special talent by lighting up the stage!

It all looked magnificent!

"Ta-dah! We're ready!" announced Moose.

A line was forming and excitement was building. Otter and Bear had the job of collecting entry fees.

"Welcome! Are you performing or watching?" asked Otter.

"There are four of us—two are watching and two are performing," said one performer.

"It's free to perform, and tickets to watch are $2 each. So, $2 plus $2. That's $4!" said Otter, giving them a reassuring hug.

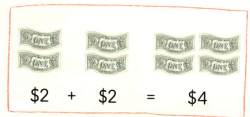

"Welcome to the show! Will you be performing?" asked Bear.

"I'm performing, and my friend is watching," replied the performer.

"One ticket to watch. That's $2 please," said Bear.

The performer handed over a $5 bill, and Bear did the math.

"Okay, $5 take away $2 is $3. Here you go!" said Bear, handing over $3 change.

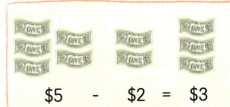

$5 - $2 = $3

The line seemed to go on forever! Money was flooding in. Otter and Bear collected the money and counted it carefully.

Owl clapped her wings together with glee, "We have a full house!"

The fireflies shone brightly to light up the stage as the musical sounds of crickets and grasshoppers filled the air. The audience looked on excitedly. The Big Talent Show was about to begin!

Owl looked smashing as she appeared from behind the curtain wearing a sparkly top hat. Into her microphone Owl announced, "Welcome to The Big Talent Show! Thank you all for coming. Now let's get our first act on stage... it's Otter!"

Otter wandered on stage, looking at the huge crowd in amazement.

"What's your talent, Otter?"

"I can do 20 jumping jacks without stopping!" said Otter.

"Great! We'd love to see this. Let's count for you, Otter!" Owl encouraged the audience to join in.

Otter started his jumping jacks, paws flying in all directions.
The crowd counted each jumping jack...

"1-2-3-4-5-6-7-8-9-10-11-12-13-14-15-16-17-18-19-20!"

Everyone clapped when Otter had finished.
Otter wiped his sweaty brow and thanked them.

Owl continued, "Next up, it's Groundhog! What is your talent?"

Groundhog pulled a toy hoop out from behind his furry back.

"I'm going to do as many twirls as I can in a minute!"

Owl smiled, "I'll start the clock. One minute is the same as 60 seconds. Your time starts NOW!"

The audience whooped as Groundhog began swirling and twirling.

They counted each one until Owl interrupted to say, "Time's up, Groundhog! How many did he do?"

"60!" The audience shouted back.

"Well, I never! 60 twirls in 60 seconds. That's a hoop every single second! Fantastic!" Owl looked very impressed.

Suddenly, a pair of antlers poked through the curtain.

"That looks like Moose... Come on, Moose! Don't be shy!" Owl encouraged.

Moose emerged nervously to thunderous applause.

"I'm going to do handstands!"

"That can't be easy with antlers. The stage is yours!" Owl opened her wing to invite Moose to take center stage.

Moose was soon doing handstands all over the place.
Finally, he collapsed in a heap, rubbing his antlers.
The crowd went crazy.

"How many did you do, Moose?
I lost count!" laughed Owl.

"That was my personal best!
32 handstands!" smiled Moose.

"Good job, Moose!"

The audience roared their approval,
having witnessed a new handstand record.

"Hang on—what's that noise?" Owl silenced the crowd to listen.

The stage curtains opened to reveal Woodpecker's beak drumming away against the stage. Tap, tap, tap.

"I'm here to do a magic trick!" said Woodpecker, pulling out a bunch of dollar bills.

"Owl, choose three dollar bills."

Owl pointed to three bills, then... poof! They disappeared. Where had they gone? The crowd looked on in wonder.

Woodpecker's beak opened to reveal one of the missing dollar bills. Wow!

"But there were three dollars!" said Owl, "Where are the other two?"

Woodpecker's wings opened to reveal a dollar bill tucked under each one.

"I still don't know how you did it! Good job, Woodpecker!"

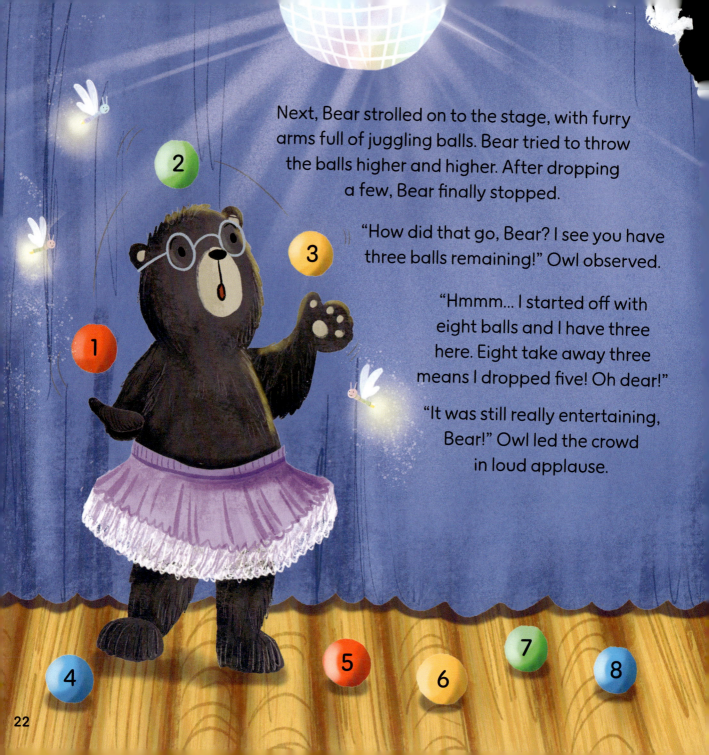

Next, Bear strolled on to the stage, with furry arms full of juggling balls. Bear tried to throw the balls higher and higher. After dropping a few, Bear finally stopped.

"How did that go, Bear? I see you have three balls remaining!" Owl observed.

"Hmmm... I started off with eight balls and I have three here. Eight take away three means I dropped five! Oh dear!"

"It was still really entertaining, Bear!" Owl led the crowd in loud applause.

And that wasn't all. Lots more amazing performers showcased all kinds of talents. There was jumping rope, singing, acting, telling jokes, playing instruments, somersaults, and dancing. There really was no end to the talent on display.

All the performers gathered on stage and the audience was quiet as Owl wrapped up the show.

"We have seen an incredible display of talent today. And we want to thank you all for sharing your different skills with us!" Owl said happily.

The audience clapped and cheered.

They were all grateful to the performers for sharing their talents on stage. What a treat to see all of the talent on display together!

After the show, the friends counted the money. They gave every performer a $1 gift, and that left them with $24 remaining.

"What should we do with all this money?" asked Bear excitedly.

"One option is to share the money between all of us," said Owl, counting it into six piles.

"Well, I really need an inflatable flamingo!" announced Otter.

"I saw some super toy hoops at the store!" Groundhog's eyes shined at the memory.

"My tired hooves would love a pair of fuzzy socks" said Moose longingly.

"I'm looking for a piggy bank to stash my dollar bills. I need to keep them safe for my magic tricks!" said Woodpecker proudly.

"And I'm definitely treating myself to a cozy blanket for the winter," Bear decided dreamily.

"Hmmm... some fine choices. But the big difference here is your wants and needs," explained Owl.

"It's all very well to want an inflatable flamingo, toy hoops, fuzzy socks, a piggy bank, and a blanket. The question is, do you really need them?"

The gang thought hard about this as Owl continued, "Wants are things you like, but you can do without. Needs are things you must have to survive, like the forest where we live, the water we drink, and the food we eat. We should always take care of our needs before our wants."

"Oh!" The group all nodded their heads as they began to understand the difference.

Owl came up with a wise plan. "I suggest we keep half of the money safely in an account at a credit union or bank. That is our savings for anything we need in the future. The rest can go toward the things we want!"

Each of the friends received $4. $2 to save for their needs, and $2 to spend on their wants. This gave them the best of both worlds!

"As long as we don't give it to Woodpecker because he makes money disappear!" said Bear.

They all laughed. The group learned they should use money to take care of their needs before their wants. And that some of the most valuable things in life—like friendship—are free!

Addition

Addition is finding the total of two or more numbers. We add things together to find the total amount. Try adding the dollar bills together. $2, add $2, equals $4.

$2 + $2 = $4

Subtraction

Subtraction is taking one number away from another number. We take away to find the amount that is left over. Try subtracting Bear's juggling balls. 8 balls, take away 5 balls, leaves 3 balls.

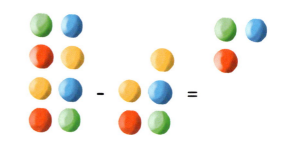

Encourage

Owl, Otter, and the gang encourage the performers with supportive words, and give them the confidence to take to the stage!

Promote

Owl, Otter, and friends put up posters that promote The Big Talent Show. These posters make others aware of the show and help to sell tickets.

Savings account

Owl, Otter, and friends plan to deposit half the money they each earned into a savings account. This will keep their money safe and help it grow until they are ready to use it.

Piggy bank

At home, you can keep your money in a piggy bank and take it out when you want to spend it. Woodpecker wants a piggy bank to store the dollar bills he uses in his magic tricks.

Wants

Owl explains that wants are things you would like to have, but can get along without. You should only consider buying things you **want** after you already have everything you **need**.

Needs

Owl explains that needs are things you must have to survive. You must make sure you have the things you **need**, like food, water, and shelter, before you spend money on things you **want**.

Written by Andrea Mills
Illustrated by Julia Seal
Design by Collaborate Ltd

Editor Becca Arlington
Designer Sif Nørskov
US Senior Editor Shannon Beatty
Jacket Designer Eleanor Bates
Publishing Assistant Francesca Harper
Production Editor Becky Fallowfield
Senior Production Controller Ena Matagic
Special Sales and Custom Publishing Executive Issy Walsh
Managing Art Editor Elle Ward
Publisher Francesca Young
Managing Director Sarah Larter

First American Edition, 2024
Published in the United States by DK Publishing
1745 Broadway, 20th Floor, New York, NY 10019

Copyright © 2024 Dorling Kindersley Limited
DK, a Division of Penguin Random House LLC
24 25 26 27 28 10 9 8 7 6 5 4 3 2 1
001–342416–Sept/2024

All rights reserved.
Without limiting the rights under the copyright reserved above, no part of this publication may be reproduced, stored in or introduced into a retrieval system, or transmitted, in any form, or by any means (electronic, mechanical, photocopying, recording, or otherwise), without the prior written permission of the copyright owner.
Published in Great Britain by Dorling Kindersley Limited

A catalog record for this book is available from the Library of Congress.
ISBN 978-0-5938-4612-4

DK books are available at special discounts when purchased in bulk for sales promotions, premiums, fund-raising, or educational use. For details, contact: DK Publishing Special Markets,
1745 Broadway, 20th Floor, New York, NY 10019
SpecialSales@dk.com

Printed and bound in Canada

www.dk.com

This book was made with Forest Stewardship Council™ certified paper – one small step in DK's commitment to a sustainable future. Learn more at www.dk.com/uk/information/sustainability